lyrics to a stranger

AF624496

Carson Yenchar

BookLeaf Publishing

Presentation by *BookLeaf Publishing*

Web: www.bookleafpub.com

E-mail: info@bookleafpub.com

ISBN: 9789395950084

First edition 2022

DEDICATION

To the ones who feel just a little odd, or dwelling in the corner, or observing from the walls of a dirty school gymnasium. You are seen, you are heard, you are loved.

ACKNOWLEDGEMENT

I would love to thank my friends for always supporting me, and for continuously providing me with inspiration, and the strength to continue pushing myself to newer heights.

I want to thank my family for supporting me through my many trials and triumphs through life, and for guiding me towards the decisions that drive me today.

And a special thanks to the outcasts and dreamers who dare to be themselves every day, despite what the world might say. Your strength and light is known and felt, and we thank you for never giving in.

PREFACE

This book came into being from the inspiration of feelings I have felt throughout my life, whether positive or negative. Both have shaped me in ways I am still navigating to this day, and it has been a long, winding road since day one. The poems I write may feel fictitious, but the words are very raw, as I hope they will be to many readers. I hope to create an impact in what I write, and hope that readers, as well as writers, will carry what is necessary for their journeys. Because no individual's journey is defined by a straight line, but rather, a plethora of curves and dead ends.

soft metal

rocking hair and silver chain,
containing the soul of rock n' roll.
hidden away lies a heart of gold,
where they're going, no one knows.

smoke billowing in heavy clouds,
parents gone and left them alone.
everyone thinks they're such a freak,
no one understands.

soft metal, stick with me,
to escape from your reality.
no one gets you like i do,
you're stronger than you know.

never let them see your fear,
learn to grow and persevere.
fight the monsters in your head,
and those who aim to kill.

two fools in love

you're a rockstar acting out,
wild and free of society.
me, i stay within the lines,
too afraid to stray.

feelings deep inside,
how could i be so blind?
didn't even realize,
what was right in front of me.

i'm an idiot in love,
with one who makes me crazy
but i like the risks i see,
so help me to be brave.

i'm an idiot in love,
with one who cares too much.
i want them to take care,
and learn to be kind to themselves.

unsteady

stumbling through ashes,
of an alternate dimension.
wondering,
how i got in this situation.

gratitude shines a light,
despite it being misplaced.
but i can't help feeling,
the irregular beat of my heart.

the ground has become unsteady,
and i'm trying to stay afloat.
their eyes drawing me closer,
and i never want to get out.

love isn't a one-way street,
yet this feels so effortless.
i want to feel steady on my feet,
but they only make me float.

years

skin torn and bleeding,
sky above a cloudy red.
pain shoots like hot flashes,
vision blurs and clears.

a year of misgivings,
finally comes to an end.
my so-called hero's journey,
drawing to a close.

i've finally stood my ground,
i didn't run away.
knowing that i became true,
gives a sense of peace.

show them the way,
teach them how to be true.
love will continue on,
that'll never change.

in suspended wires

everything freezes,
movement sways and stills.
dizzying satisfaction,
regarding what lies before me.

ears buzzing,
fading in and out.
blending together,
until it meshes.

wires suspend me,
air tightens around me.
such sickening force,
but i'm ready to let go.

sadness and anger overwhelms,
mixed with happiness.
granted a sad type of happy,
feelings i'll never forget.

s.a.d.

let me wallow in darkness,
my one and true companion.
holding me through tears,
until i pass out from exhaustion.

get up off your knees,
and walk away from me.
don't need your pretty excuses,
to know how ashamed i feel inside.

what's there to be sad about,
i'll give you a hundred reasons.
that would hold me up,
and carry me away.

don't try to give me advice,
on how to be more content.
i'm living the narrative,
until existence is over.

losing resistance

am i the one holding back,
due to the buried truth?
the truth i've been afraid to face,
that no one ever knew.

you make me wanna blossom,
into someone i've never met.
you're so different,
yet you keep me coming back.

lost all my resistance,
to the urges driving me now.
wild and dangerous,
but in the best possible way.

i'll explore your darkest corners,
tuck your hair behind your ear.
love you until we're gone,
upon a trail of light.

glass walls

light reflects and bends,
beneath prisms of crystal.
bronze eyes piercing through,
nothing in their empty gaze.

hold on to my gaze,
as we navigate the staircase.
straight up to the galaxies,
twirling in dizzying wonder.

pieces apart,
reassembled again into weaker form.
wobbling on an unsteady frame,
close to toppling over.

you can be afraid,
but don't let it consume you.
fear can flow like toxic fumes,
until it overfills.

through the window pane

i tumble into wispy wings,
as i fear what tomorrow may bring.
never knowing what life could be,
if i were allowed to be free.

i see glass shine through my eyes,
yet can't help but despise.
it mocks and glows and sits,
then cold reality hits.

on that endless window pane,
goes round and round and back again.
want to let go but what's the use?
can't seem to allow my feelings loose.

if a window loses all its glass,
or the soil made without the grass.
would it mean much more or less,
guess i'll always be a mess.

eye contact

it's intimate, they say,
when one eye meets another.
or it can be pure agony,
for some others.

connection means direction,
and eyes seal the deal.
if the ground is all to see,
what's the point of connection?

i don't mean to appear distracted,
nor dazed by specks of dust.
i just fear what will happen,
once iris touches iris.

it means something deep,
the meeting of one's eyes.
but if that's all there is,
what about everything else?

holding onto (nothing at all)

holding on at such a cost,
my fist wrapped around ghostly leather.
piercing through the slick, cold matter,
feeling nothing at all.

what a cost i can't pay,
wasting a life, wasting away.
holding on to space that's fake,
no objects to consider.

nothing feels like inhaling,
the exhale light years behind.
blackness coating surfaces,
that were never there at all.

wishing i could let go,
maybe i already have.
cause what's there to hold onto,
when there's nothing there at all?

queen of sleeping

upon a throne of bed sheets,
lies a pale woman.
staring up towards the ceiling,
hoping to catch the stars.

no thoughts,
but at the same time too many.
wasting away her days,
with no future to behold.

too tired to work,
frankly too tired to care.
the crown leans too far to the edge,
toppling into coarse carpet.

the woman merely shrugs,
wan smile upon her cheeks.
closed eyes sink deeper,
and she sleeps.

spout bursts

overwhelming growth,
no red lights in sight.
can't control feelings too strong,
too crowded.

bursts of flames,
lit by liquid gasoline.
heat unbearable to face,
the shame too maddening to erase.

control it they say,
to something they can't understand.
do you not think,
that i have tried?

bursts grow unable to redeem,
for others and for me.
wish it was easy to erase,
but the growth continues.

blame me

everything seems to fall on me,
and i'm left with piles of regret.
blame feels like stones in my pocket,
i never seem to have enough.

nothing feels right,
like a raven floating in darkness.
impending doom looms high,
and i'm never ready.

blaming me is easier,
all the cards against me.
can't feel upset about anything,
when it affects everyone else.

blame me all you want,
but i am still human.
kick the stones further down,
but holes have begun forming.

theatre blues

remember when the lights went up,
the stage humid and chipped.
heavy curtains and the smell of paint,
laughter ringing out.

nerves charged at maximum,
disperse upon entry.
friends gathered in harmony,
and it feels like a reunion.

never forget those times,
feeling a calm so resound.
like coming back from darkness,
after years of hurt and pain.

moving on and forward,
parting ways to pursue life.
but the memories still remain,
and continue to spread through time.

confusing rainbow

learning to be accepting,
is the hardest lesson.
accepting yourself completely,
an entirely different challenge.

incomplete in structure,
getting things mixed and twisted.
feeling wrong for wanting,
never getting answers.

the want to speak up,
gets suffocated by doubt.
is it fake or concrete,
is never fully known.

will there ever be content,
in half-made conclusions?
suppose that's what life is for,
figuring out the true conclusion.

hyperfixation

people are quick to judge,
especially trivial things.
such as hobbies and interests,
they barely understand.

happiness takes many forms,
for some it's fiction and fantasy.
an escape from reality,
that is always unforgiving.

why speak hate towards others,
doing what they love?
if it has such an impact,
then why are you still standing?

let others love what they love,
and spread their excitement.
cause everyone deserves a moment,
away from dull existence.

moonlight (with you)

what is this feeling,
suffocating yet freeing?
leading me away,
from the conventions of controlled life.

i'm breaking through the cage,
and into your gaze.
flowing river of thought,
reduced to mumbled nonsense.

my passions have never seemed so far,
and yet so very near.
now you're here,
taking my everlasting breath.

moonlight shines upon you,
like a blanket full of stars.
you never have to hold back with me,
cause all i see is the best.

where stars hide

tucked within the pages,
of dust-covered oak.
with dust comes more dust,
dancing through filtered light.

pearly vase in the corner,
gives a luminescent sheen.
my eyes track the room,
a habit born out of trauma.

the toe of my shoe hits the light,
faded leather glittering dully.
i pretend it is the sun,
a warmth engulfing.

almost like a rare hug from a father,
still the stars burn and die.
but there are still stars,
hidden within crevices of shadows.

inner beauty

society chooses to believe,
that full lips and curvy waist define.
that a full head of hair and smooth skin,
are what keeps us alive.

but what happened to words,
wound with vines and roses?
or boisterous laughter,
echoing down alleys?

smiles that spread open,
like a love letter.
dancing in the rain,
silhouettes framed in street lights.

opening up for the ones we love,
the reciprocation awakening.
you can never really know another,
by looking at the outer frame.

bind the spine

needles thread the stitch,
weaving through interlocks.
gaining speed with each pull,
but at what cost?

if it loosens over time,
how will the spine keep up?
it will unravel and flatten,
leaving remains of a soul.

slow and steady,
that's how the saying goes.
the threads stretched too thin,
the more likely to snap.

pull taut on the wool,
connecting the pieces.
for a spine keeps one together,
without really knowing why.

www.ingramcontent.com/pod-product-compliance
Lightning Source LLC
Chambersburg PA
CBHW051719130826
49812CB00034B/1255
* 9 7 8 9 3 9 5 9 5 0 0 8 4 *